higher-level thinking
Questions
Developing Character

questions by
Miguel Kagan

created and designed by
Miguel Kagan

illustrated by
Celso Rodriguez

Kagan

Kagan Publishing

981 Calle Amanecer

San Clemente, CA 92673

(949) 545-6300

Fax: (949) 545-6301

1 (800) 933-2667

www.KaganOnline.com

ISBN: 978-1-879097-54-4

Table of ❓ Contents

> **I had six
> honest serving men
> They taught me all I knew:
> Their names were Where
> and What and When
> and Why and How and
> Who.**
>
> — Rudyard Kipling

Higher-Level Thinking Questions for Developing Character
Kagan Publishing • 1 (800) 933-2667 • www.KaganOnline.com

Introduction

In your hands you hold a powerful book. It is a member of a series of transformative blackline activity books. Between the covers, you will find questions, questions, and more questions! But these are no ordinary questions. These are the important kind—higher-level thinking questions—the kind that stretch your students' minds; the kind that release your students' natural curiosity about the world; the kind that rack your students' brains; the kind that instill in your students a sense of wonderment about your curriculum.

But we are getting a bit ahead of ourselves. Let's start from the beginning. Since this is a book of questions, it seems only appropriate for this introduction to pose a few questions—about the book and its underlying educational philosophy. So Mr. Kipling's Six Honest Serving Men, if you will, please lead the way:

What?
What are higher-level thinking questions?

This is a loaded question (as should be all good questions). Using our analytic thinking skills, let's break this question down into two smaller questions: 1) What is higher-level thinking? and 2) What are questions? When we understand the types of thinking skills and the types of questions, we can combine the best of both worlds, crafting beautiful questions to generate the range of higher-level thinking in our students!

Types of Thinking

There are many different types of thinking. Some types of thinking include:

- applying
- associating
- comparing
- contrasting
- defining
- elaborating
- empathizing
- experimenting
- generalizing
- investigating
- making analogies
- planning
- prioritizing
- recalling
- reflecting
- reversing
- sequencing
- summarizing
- synthesizing
- assessing
- augmenting
- connecting
- decision-making
- drawing conclusions
- eliminating
- evaluating
- explaining
- inferring consequences
- inventing
- memorizing
- predicting
- problem-solving
- reducing
- relating
- role-taking
- substituting
- symbolizing
- understanding
- thinking about thinking (metacognition)

This is quite a formidable list. It's nowhere near complete. Thinking is a big, multifaceted phenomenon. Perhaps the most widely recognized system for classifying thinking and classroom questions is Benjamin Bloom's Taxonomy of Thinking Skills. Bloom's Taxonomy classifies thinking skills into six hierarchical levels. It begins with the lower levels of thinking skills and moves up to higher-level thinking skills: 1) Knowledge, 2) Comprehension, 3) Application, 4) Analysis, 5) Synthesis, 6) Evaluation. See Bloom's Taxonomy on the following page.

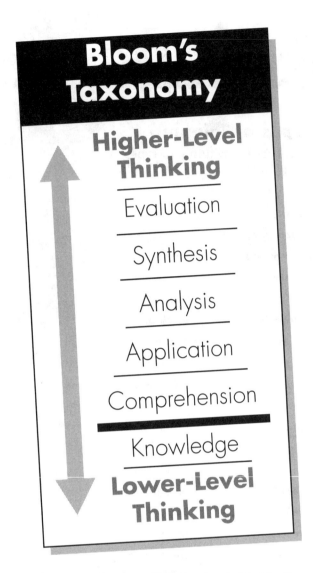

Bloom's Taxonomy

Higher-Level Thinking

Evaluation

Synthesis

Analysis

Application

Comprehension

Knowledge

Lower-Level Thinking

In education, the term "higher-level thinking" often refers to the higher levels of Mr. Bloom's taxonomy. But Bloom's Taxonomy is but one way of organizing and conceptualizing the various types of thinking skills.

There are many ways we can cut the thinking skills pie. We can alternatively view the many different types of thinking skills as, well…many different skills. Some thinking skills may be hierarchical. Some may be interrelated. And some may be relatively independent.

In this book, we take a pragmatic, functional approach. Each type of thinking skill serves a different function. So called "lower-level" thinking skills are very useful for certain purposes. Memorizing and understanding information are

invaluable skills that our students will use throughout their lives. But so too are many of the "higher-level" thinking skills on our list. The more facets of students' thinking skills we develop, the better we prepare them for lifelong success.

Because so much classroom learning heretofore has focused on the "lower rungs" of the thinking skills ladder—knowledge and comprehension, or memorization and understanding—in this series of books we have chosen to focus on questions to generate "higher-level" thinking. This book is an attempt to correct the imbalance in the types of thinking skills developed by classroom questions.

Types of Questions
As we ask questions of our students, we further promote cognitive development when we use Fat questions, Low-Consensus questions, and True questions.

Fat Questions vs. Skinny Questions
Skinny questions are questions that require a skinny answer. For example, after reading a poem, we can ask: "Did you like the poem?" Even though this question could be categorized as an Evaluation question—Bloom's highest level of thinking— it can be answered with one monosyllabic word: "Yes" or "No." How much thinking are we actually generating in our students?

We can reframe this question to make it a fat question: "What things did you like about the poem? What things did you dislike?" Notice no short answer will do. Answering this fattened-up question requires more elaboration. These fat questions presuppose not that there is only one thing but things plural that the student liked and things that she did not like. Making things plural is one way to make skinny questions fat. Students stretch their minds to come up with multiple ideas or solutions. Other easy ways to make questions fat is to add "Why or why not?" or "Explain" or "Describe" or "Defend your position" to the end of a question. These additions promote elaboration beyond a skinny answer. Because language and thought are intimately intertwined, questions that require elaborate responses stretch students' thinking: They grapple to articulate their thoughts.

The type of questions we ask impact not just the type of thinking we develop in our students, but also the depth of thought. Fat questions elicit fat responses. Fat responses develop both depth of thinking and range of thinking skills. The questions in this book are designed to elicit fat responses—deep and varied thinking.

High-Consensus Questions vs. Low-Consensus Questions

A high-consensus question is one to which most people would give the same response, usually a right or wrong answer. After learning about sound, we can ask our students: "What is the name of a room specially designed to improve acoustics for the audience?" This is a high-consensus question. The answer (auditorium) is either correct or incorrect.

Compare the previous question with a low-consensus question: "If you were going to build an auditorium, what special design features would you take into consideration?" Notice, to the low-consensus question there is no right or wrong answer. Each person formulates his or her unique response. To answer, students must apply what they learned, use their ingenuity and creativity.

High-consensus questions promote convergent thinking. With high-consensus questions we strive to direct students *what to think*. Low-consensus questions promote divergent thinking, both critical and creative. With low-consen-

sus questions we strive to develop students' *ability to think*. The questions in this book are low-consensus questions designed to promote independent, critical and creative thought.

True Questions vs. Review Questions

We all know what review questions are. They're the ones in the back of every chapter and unit. Review questions ask students to regurgitate previously stated or learned information. For example, after learning about the rain forest we may ask: "What percent of the world's oxygen does the rain forest produce?" Students can go back a few pages in their books or into their memory banks and pull out the answer. This is great if we are working on memorization skills, but does little to develop "higher-order" thinking skills.

True questions, on the other hand, are meaningful questions—questions to which we do not know the answer. For example: "What might happen if all the world's rain forests were cut down?" This is a hypothetical; we don't know the answer but considering the question forces us to think. We infer some logical consequences based on what we know. The goal of true questions is not a correct answer, but the thinking journey students take to create a meaningful response. True questions are more representative of real life. Seldom is there a black and white answer. In life, we struggle with ambiguity, confounding variables, and uncertain outcomes. There are millions of shades of gray. True questions prepare students to deal with life's uncertainties.

When we ask a review question, we know the answer and are checking to see if the student does also. When we ask a true question, it is truly a question. We don't necessarily know the answer and neither does the student. True

> Education is not the filling of a pail, but the lighting of a fire.
> — William Butler Yeats

Types of Questions

Skinny ➡ **Fat**

Skinny	**Fat**
• Short Answer	• Elaborated Answer
• Shallow Thinking	• Deep Thinking

High-Consensus ➡ **Low-Consensus**

High-Consensus	**Low-Consensus**
• Right or Wrong Answer	• No Single Correct Answer
• Develops Convergent Thinking	• Develops Divergent Thinking
• "What" to Think	• "How" to Think

Review ➡ **True**

Review	**True**
• Asker Knows Answer	• Asker Doesn't Know Answer
• Checking for Correctness	• Invitation to Think

questions are often an invitation to think, ponder, speculate, and engage in a questioning process.

We can use true questions in the classroom to make our curriculum more personally meaningful, to promote investigation, and awaken students' sense of awe and wonderment in what we teach. Many questions you will find in this book are true questions designed to make the content provocative, intriguing, and personally relevant.

The box above summarizes the different types of questions. The questions you will find in this book are a move away from skinny, high-consensus, review questions toward fat, low-consensus true questions. As we ask these types of questions in our class, we transform even mundane content into a springboard for higher-level thinking. As we integrate these question gems into our daily lessons, we create powerful learning experiences. ***We do not fill our students' pails with knowledge; we kindle their fires to become lifetime thinkers.***

Why?
Why should I use higher-level thinking questions in my classroom?

As we enter the new millennium, major shifts in our economic structure are changing the ways we work and live. The direction is increasingly toward an information-based, high-tech economy. The sum of our technological information is exploding. We could give you a figure how rapidly information is doubling, but by the time you read this, the number would be outdated! No kidding.

But this is no surprise. This is our daily reality. We see it around us everyday and on the news: cloning, gene manipulation, e-mail, the Internet, Mars rovers, electric cars, hybrids, laser surgery, CD-ROMs, DVDs. All around us we see the wheels of progress turning: New discoveries, new technologies, a new societal knowledge and information base. New jobs are being created

Higher-Level Thinking Questions for Developing Character
Kagan Publishing • 1 (800) 933-2667 • www.KaganOnline.com

today in fields that simply didn't exist yesterday.

How do we best prepare our students for this uncertain future—a future in which the only constant will be change? As we are propelled into a world of ever-increasing change, what is the relative value of teaching students facts versus thinking skills? This point becomes even more salient when we realize that students cannot master everything, and many facts will soon become obsolete. Facts become outdated or irrelevant. Thinking skills are for a lifetime. Increasingly, how we define educational success will be away from the quantity of information mastered. Instead, we will define success as our students' ability to generate questions, apply, synthesize, predict, evaluate, compare, categorize.

If we as a professionals are to proactively respond to these societal shifts, thinking skills will become central to our curriculum. Whether we teach thinking skills directly, or we integrate them into our curriculum, the power to think is the greatest gift we can give our students!

We believe the questions you will find in this book are a step in the direction of preparing students for lifelong success. The goal is to develop independent thinkers who are critical and creative, regardless of the content. We hope the books in this series are more than sets of questions. We provide them as a model approach to questioning in the classroom.

On pages 8 and 9, you will find Questions to Engage Students' Thinking Skills. These pages contain numerous types of thinking and questions designed to engage each thinking skill. As you make your own questions for your students with your own content, use these question starters to help you frame your

---

Virtually the only predictable trend is continuing change.

— Dr. Linda Tsantis, Creating the Future

---

questions to stimulate various facets of your students' thinking skills. Also let your students use these question starters to generate their own higher-level thinking questions about the curriculum.

Who?
Who is this book for?

This book is for you and your students, but mostly for your students. It is designed to help make your job easier. Inside you will find hundreds of ready-to-use reproducible questions. Sometimes in the press for time we opt for what is easy over what is best. These books attempt to make easy what is best. In this treasure chest, you will find hours and hours of timesaving ready-made questions and activities.

Place Higher-Level Thinking In Your Students' Hands

As previously mentioned, this book is even more for your students than for you. As teachers, we ask a tremendous number of questions. Primary teachers ask 3.5 to 6.5 questions per minute! Elementary teachers average 348 questions a day. How many questions would you predict our students ask? Researchers asked this question. What they found was shocking: Typical students ask approximately one question per month.* One question per month!

Although this study may not be representative of your classroom, it does suggest that in general, as teachers we are missing out on a very powerful force—student-generated questions. The capacity to answer higher-level thinking questions is a

---

* Myra & David Sadker, "Questioning Skills" in *Classroom Teaching Skills*, 2nd ed. Lexington, MA: D.C. Heath & Co., 1982.

Questions to Engage Students' Thinking Skills

Analyzing
- How could you break down…?
- What components…?
- What qualities/characteristics…?

Applying
- How is _____ an example of…?
- What practical applications…?
- What examples…?
- How could you use…?
- How does this apply to…?
- In your life, how would you apply…?

Assessing
- By what criteria would you assess…?
- What grade would you give…?
- How could you improve…?

Augmenting/Elaborating
- What ideas might you add to…?
- What more can you say about…?

Categorizing/Classifying/Organizing
- How might you classify…?
- If you were going to categorize…?

Comparing/Contrasting
- How would you compare…?
- What similarities…?
- What are the differences between…?
- How is _____ different…?

Connecting/Associating
- What do you already know about…?
- What connections can you make between…?
- What things do you think of when you think of…?

Decision-Making
- How would you decide…?
- If you had to choose between…?

Defining
- How would you define…?
- In your own words, what is…?

Describing/Summarizing
- How could you describe/summarize…?
- If you were a reporter, how would you describe…?

Determining Cause/Effect
- What is the cause of…?
- How does _____ effect _____?
- What impact might…?

Drawing Conclusions/ Inferring Consequences
- What conclusions can you draw from…?
- What would happen if…?
- What would have happened if…?
- If you changed _____, what might happen?

Eliminating
- What part of _____ might you eliminate?
- How could you get rid of…?

Evaluating
- What is your opinion about…?
- Do you prefer…?
- Would you rather…?
- What is your favorite…?
- Do you agree or disagree…?
- What are the positive and negative aspects of…?
- What are the advantages and disadvantages…?
- If you were a judge…?
- On a scale of 1 to 10, how would you rate…?
- What is the most important…?
- Is it better or worse…?

Explaining
- How can you explain…?
- What factors might explain…?

Higher-Level Thinking Questions for Developing Character
Kagan Publishing • 1 (800) 933-2667 • www.KaganOnline.com

Experimenting
- How could you test...?
- What experiment could you do to...?

Generalizing
- What general rule can...?
- What principle could you apply...?
- What can you say about all...?

Interpreting
- Why is _____ important?
- What is the significance of...?
- What role...?
- What is the moral of...?

Inventing
- What could you invent to...?
- What machine could...?

Investigating
- How could you find out more about...?
- If you wanted to know about...?

Making Analogies
- How is _____ like _____?
- What analogy can you invent for...?

Observing
- What observations did you make about...?
- What changes...?

Patterning
- What patterns can you find...?
- How would you describe the organization of...?

Planning
- What preparations would you...?

Predicting/Hypothesizing
- What would you predict...?
- What is your theory about...?
- If you were going to guess...?

Prioritizing
- What is more important...?
- How might you prioritize...?

Problem-Solving
- How would you approach the problem?
- What are some possible solutions to...?

Reducing/Simplifying
- In a word, how would you describe...?
- How can you simplify...?

Reflecting/Metacognition
- What would you think if...?
- How can you describe what you were thinking when...?

Relating
- How is _____ related to _____?
- What is the relationship between...?
- How does _____ depend on _____?

Reversing/Inversing
- What is the opposite of...?

Role-Taking/Empathizing
- If you were (someone/something else)...?
- How would you feel if...?

Sequencing
- How could you sequence...?
- What steps are involved in...?

Substituting
- What could have been used instead of...?
- What else could you use for...?
- What might you substitute for...?
- What is another way...?

Symbolizing
- How could you draw...?
- What symbol best represents...?

Synthesizing
- How could you combine...?
- What could you put together...?

wonderful skill we can give our students, as is the skill to solve problems. Arguably more important skills are the ability to find problems to solve and formulate questions to answer. If we look at the great thinkers of the world—the Einsteins, the Edisons, the Freuds—their thinking is marked by a yearning to solve tremendous questions and problems. It is this questioning process that distinguishes those who illuminate and create our world from those who merely accept it.

Make Learning an Interactive Process

Higher-level thinking is not just something that occurs between students' ears! Students benefit from an interactive process. This basic premise underlies the majority of activities you will find in this book.

As students discuss questions and listen to others, they are confronted with differing perspectives and are pushed to articulate their own thinking well beyond the level they could attain on their own. Students too have an enormous capacity to mediate each other's learning. When we heterogeneously group students to work together, we create an environment to move students through their zone of proximal development. We also provide opportunities for tutoring and leadership. Verbal interaction with peers in cooperative groups adds a dimension to questions not available with whole-class questions and answers.

> **Asking a good question requires students to think harder than giving a good answer.**
> — Robert Fisher, Teaching Children to Learn

Reflect on this analogy: If we wanted to teach our students to catch and throw, we could bring in one tennis ball and take turns throwing it to each student and having them throw it back to us. Alternatively, we could bring in twenty balls and have our students form small groups and have them toss the ball back and forth to each other. Picture the two classrooms: One with twenty balls being caught at any one moment, and the other with just one. In which class would students better and more quickly learn to catch and throw?

The same is true with thinking skills. When we make our students more active participants in the learning process, they are given dramatically more opportunities to produce their own thought and to strengthen their own thinking skills. Would you rather have one question being asked and answered at any one moment in your class, or twenty? Small groups mean more questioning and more thinking. Instead of rarely answering a teacher question or rarely generating their own question, asking and answering questions becomes a regular part of your students' day. It is through cooperative interaction that we truly turn our classroom into a higher-level think tank. The associated personal and social benefits are invaluable.

When?

When do I use higher-level thinking questions?

Do I use these questions at the beginning of the lesson, during the lesson, or after? The answer, of course, is all of the above.

Use these questions or your own thinking questions at the beginning of the lesson to provide a motivational set for the lesson. Pique students' interest about the content with some provocative questions: "What would happen if we didn't have gravity?" "Why did Pilgrims get along with some Native Americans, but not others?" "What do you think this book will be about?" Make the content personally relevant by bringing in students' own knowledge, experiences, and feelings about the content: "What do you know about spiders?" "What things do you like about mystery stories?" "How would you feel if explorers invaded your land and killed your family?" "What do you wonder about electricity?"

Use the higher-level thinking questions throughout your lessons. Use the many questions and activities in this book not as a replacement of your curriculum, but as an additional avenue to explore the content and stretch students' thinking skills.

Use the questions after your lesson. Use the higher-level thinking questions, a journal writing activity, or the question starters as an extension activity to your lesson or unit.

Or just use the questions as stand-alone sponge activities for students or teams who have finished their work and need a challenging project to work on.

It doesn't matter when you use them, just use them frequently. As questioning becomes a habitual part of the classroom day, students' fear of asking silly questions is diminished. As the ancient Chinese proverb states, "Those who ask a silly question may seem a fool for five minutes, but those who do not ask remain a fool for life."

The important thing is to never stop questioning.

— Albert Einstein

As teachers, we should make a conscious effort to ensure that a portion of the many questions we ask on a daily basis are those that move our students beyond rote memorization. When we integrate higher-level thinking questions into our daily lessons, we transform our role from transmitters of knowledge to engineers of learning.

Where?

Where should I keep this book?

Keep it close by. Inside there are 16 sets of questions. Pull it out any time you teach these topics or need a quick, easy, fun activity or journal writing topic.

How?
How do I get the most out of this book?

In this book you will find 16 topics arranged alphabetically. For each topic there are reproducible pages for: 1) 16 Question Cards, 2) a Journal Writing activity page, 3) and a Question Starters activity page.

1. Question Cards

The Question Cards are truly the heart of this book. There are numerous ways the Question Cards can be used. After the other activity pages are introduced, you will find a description of a variety of engaging formats to use the Question Cards.

Specific and General Questions

Some of the questions provided in this book series are content-specific and others are content-free. For example, the literature questions in the Literature books are content-specific. Questions for the Great Kapok Tree deal specifically with that literature selection. Some language arts questions in the Language Arts book, on the other hand, are content-free. They are general questions that can be used over and over again with new content. For example, the Book Review questions can be used after reading any book. The Story Structure questions can be used after reading any story. You can tell by glancing at the title of the set and some of the questions whether the set is content-specific or content-free.

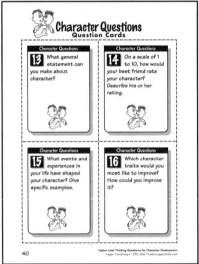

A Little Disclaimer

Not all of the "questions" on the Question Cards are actually questions. Some instruct students to do something. For example, "Compare and contrast…" We can also use these directives to develop the various facets of students' thinking skills.

The Power of Think Time

As you and your students use these questions, don't forget about the power of Think Time! There are two different think times. The first is the time between the question and the response. The second is the time between the response and feedback on the response. Think time has been shown to greatly enhance the quality of student thinking. If students are not pausing for either think time, or doing it too briefly, emphasize its importance. Five little seconds of silent think time after the question and five more seconds before feedback are proven, powerful ways to promote higher-level thinking in your class.

Use Your Question Cards for Years

For attractive Question Cards that will last for years, photocopy them on color card-stock paper and laminate them. To save time, have the Materials Monitor from each team pick up one card set, a pair of scissors for the team, and an envelope or rubber band. Each team cuts out their own set of Question Cards. When they are done with the activity, students can place the Question Cards in the envelope and write the name of the set on the envelope or wrap the cards with a rubber band for storage.

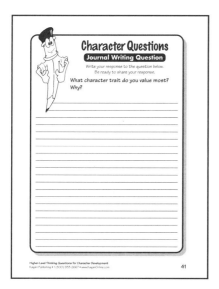

2. Journal Question

The Journal Writing page contains one of the 16 questions as a journal writing prompt. You can substitute any question, or use one of your own. The power of journal writing cannot be overstated. The act of writing takes longer than speaking and thinking. It allows the brain time to make deep connections to the content. Writing requires the writer to present his or her response in a clear, concise language. Writing develops both strong thinking and communication skills.

A helpful activity before journal writing is to have students discuss the question in pairs or in small teams. Students discuss their ideas and what they plan to write. This little prewriting activity ignites ideas for those students who stare blankly at their Journal Writing page. The interpersonal interaction further helps students articulate what they are thinking about the topic and invites students to delve deeper into the topic.

Tell students before they write that they will share their journal entries with a partner or with their team. This motivates many students to improve their entry. Sharing written responses also promotes flexible thinking with open-ended questions, and allows students to hear their peers' responses, ideas and writing styles.

Have students keep a collection of their journal entries in a three-ring binder. This way you can collect them if you wish for assessment or have students go back to reflect on their own learning. If you are using questions across the curriculum, each subject can have its own journal or own section within the binder. Use the provided blackline on the following page for a cover for students' journals or have students design their own.

3. Question Starters

The Question Starters activity page is designed to put the questions in the hands of your students. Use these question starters to scaffold your students' ability to write their own thinking questions. This page includes eight question starters to direct students to generate questions across the levels and types of thinking. This Question Starters activity page can be used in a few different ways:

Individual Questions

Have students independently come up with their own questions. When done, they can trade their questions with a partner. On a separate sheet of paper students answer their partners' questions. After answering, partners can share how they answered each other's questions.

JOURNAL

My Best Thinking

_____

This Journal Belongs to

Higher-Level Thinking Questions for Developing Character
Kagan Publishing • 1 (800) 933-2667 • www.KaganOnline.com

Pair Questions

Students work in pairs to generate questions to send to another pair. Partners take turns writing each question and also take turns recording each answer. After answering, pairs pair up to share how they answered each other's questions.

Team Questions

Students work in teams to generate questions to send to another team. Teammates take turns writing each question and recording each answer. After answering, teams pair up to share how they answered each other's questions.

Teacher-Led Questions

For young students, lead the whole class in coming up with good higher-level thinking questions.

Teach Your Students About Thinking and Questions

An effective tool to improve students' thinking skills is to teach students about the types of thinking skills and types of questions. Teaching students about the types of thinking skills improves their metacognitive abilities. When students are aware of the types of thinking, they may more effectively plan, monitor, and evaluate their own thinking. When students understand the types of questions and the basics of question construction, they are more likely to create effective higher-level thinking questions. In doing so they develop their own thinking skills and the thinking of classmates as they work to answer each other's questions.

Table of Activities

The Question Cards can be used in a variety of game-like formats to forge students' thinking skills. They can be used for cooperative team and pair work, for whole-class questioning, for independent activities, or at learning centers. On the following pages you will find numerous excellent options to use your Question Cards. As you use the Question Cards in this book, try the different activities listed below to add novelty and variety to the higher-level thinking process.

Activities

team activity #1

Question Commander

Preferably in teams of four, students shuffle their Question Cards and place them in a stack, questions facing down, so that all teammates can easily reach the Question Cards. Give each team a Question Commander set of instructions (blackline provided on following page) to lead them through each question.

Student One becomes the Question Commander for the first question. The Question Commander reads the question aloud to the team, then asks the teammates to think about the question and how they would answer it. After the think time, the Question Commander selects a teammate to answer the question. The Question Commander can spin a spinner or roll a die to select who will answer. After the teammate gives the answer, Question Commander again calls for think time, this time asking the team to think about the answer. After the think time, the Question Commander leads a team discus-

sion in which any teammember can contribute his or her thoughts or ideas to the question, or give praise or reactions to the answer.

When the discussion is over, Student Two becomes the Question Commander for the next question.

Question Commander
Instruction Cards

Question Commander

1. Ask the Question:
Question Commander reads the question to the team.
2. Think Time: "Think of your best answer."
3. Answer the Question:
The Question Commander selects a teammate to answer the question.
4. Think Time: "Think about how you would answer differently or add to the answer."
5. Team Discussion: As a team, discuss other possible answers or reactions to the answer given.

Question Commander

1. Ask the Question:
Question Commander reads the question to the team.
2. Think Time: "Think of your best answer."
3. Answer the Question:
The Question Commander selects a teammate to answer the question.
4. Think Time: "Think about how you would answer differently or add to the answer."
5. Team Discussion: As a team, discuss other possible answers or reactions to the answer given.

Question Commander

1. Ask the Question:
Question Commander reads the question to the team.
2. Think Time: "Think of your best answer."
3. Answer the Question:
The Question Commander selects a teammate to answer the question.
4. Think Time: "Think about how you would answer differently or add to the answer."
5. Team Discussion: As a team, discuss other possible answers or reactions to the answer given.

Question Commander

1. Ask the Question:
Question Commander reads the question to the team.
2. Think Time: "Think of your best answer."
3. Answer the Question:
The Question Commander selects a teammate to answer the question.
4. Think Time: "Think about how you would answer differently or add to the answer."
5. Team Discussion: As a team, discuss other possible answers or reactions to the answer given.

Fan-N-Pick

In a team of four, Student One fans out the question cards, and says, "Pick a card, any card!" Student Two picks a card and reads the question out loud to teammates. After five seconds of think time, Student Three gives his or her answer. After another five seconds of think time, Student Four paraphrases, praises, or adds to the answer given. Students rotate roles for each new round.

Spin-N-Think

Spin-N-Think spinners are available from Kagan to lead teams through the steps of higher-level thinking. Students spin the Spin-N-Think™ spinner to select a student at each stage of the questioning to: 1) ask the question, 2) answer the question, 3) paraphrase and praise the answer, 4) augment the answer, and 5) discuss the question or answer. The Spin-N-Think™ game makes higher-level thinking more fun, and holds students accountable because they are often called upon, but never know when their number will come up.

Three-Step Interview

After the question is read to the team, students pair up. The first step is an interview in which one student interviews the other about the question. In the second step, students remain with their partner but switch roles: The interviewer becomes the interviewee. In the third step, the pairs come back together and each student in turn presents to the team what their partner shared. Three-Step Interview is strong for individual accountability, active listening, and paraphrasing skills.

Team Discussion

Team Discussion is an easy and informal way of processing the questions: Students read a question and then throw it open for discussion. Team Discussion, however, does not ensure that there is individual accountability or equal participation.

Think-Pair-Square

One student reads a question out loud to teammates. Partners on the same side of the table then pair up to discuss the question and their answers. Then, all four students come together for an open discussion about the question.

Question-Write-RoundRobin

Students take turns asking the team the question. After each question is asked, each student writes his or her ideas on a piece of paper. After students have finished writing, in turn they share their ideas. This format creates strong individual accountability because each student is expected to develop and share an answer for every question.

Mix-Pair-Discuss

Each student gets a different Question Card. For 16 to 32 students, use two sets of questions. In this case, some students may have the same question which is OK. Students get out of their seats and mix around the classroom. They pair up with a partner. One partner reads his or her Question Card and the other answers. Then they switch roles. When done they trade cards and find a new partner. The process is repeated for a predetermined amount of time. The rule is students cannot pair up with the same partner twice. Students may get the same questions twice or more, but each time it is with a new partner. This strategy is a fun, energizing way to ask and answer questions.

Think-Pair-Share

Think-Pair-Share is teacher-directed. The teacher asks the question, then gives students think time. Students then pair up to share their thoughts about the question. After the pair discussion, one student is called on to share with the class what was shared in his or her pair. Think-Pair-Share does not provide as much active participation for students as Think-Pair-Square because only one student is called upon at a time, but is a nice way to do whole-class sharing.

Inside-Outside Circle

Each student gets a Question Card. Half of the students form a circle facing out. The other half forms a circle around the inside circle; each student in the outside circle faces one student in the inside circle. Students in the outside circle ask inside circle students a question. After the inside circle students answer the question, students switch roles questioning and answering. After both have asked and answered a question, they each praise the other's answers and then hold up a hand indicating they are finished. When most students have a hand up, have students trade cards with their partner and rotate to a new partner. To rotate, tell the outside circle to move to the left. This format is a lively and enjoyable way to ask questions and have students listen to the thinking of many classmates.

Question & Answer

This might sound familiar: Instead of giving students the Question Cards, the teacher asks the questions and calls on one student at a time to answer. This traditional format eliminates simultaneous, cooperative interaction, but may be good for introducing younger students to higher-level questions.

Higher-Level Thinking Questions for Developing Character
Kagan Publishing • 1 (800) 933-2667 • www.KaganOnline.com

Numbered Heads Together

Students number off in their teams so that every student has a number. The teacher asks a question. Students put their "heads together" to discuss the question. The teacher then calls on a number and selects a student with that number to share what his or her team discussed.

RallyRobin

Each pair gets a set of Question Cards. Student A in the pair reads the question out loud to his or her partner. Student B answers. Partners take turns asking and answering each question.

Pair Discussion

Partners take turns asking the question. The pair then discusses the answer together. Unlike RallyRobin, students discuss the answer. Both students contribute to answering and to discussing each other's ideas.

Question-Write-Share-Discuss

One partner reads the Question Card out loud to his or her teammate. Both students write down their ideas. Partners take turns sharing what they wrote. Partners discuss how their ideas are similar and different.

Journal Writing

Students pick one Question Card and make a journal entry or use the question as the prompt for an essay or creative writing. Have students share their writing with a partner or in turn with teammates.

Independent Answers

Students each get their own set of Questions Cards. Pairs or teams can share a set of questions, or the questions can be written on the board or put on the overhead projector. Students work by themselves to answer the questions on a separate sheet of paper. When done, students can compare their answers with a partner, teammates, or the whole class.

Center Ideas

1. Question Card Center

At one center, have the Question Cards and a Spin-N-Think™ spinner, Question Commander instruction card, or Fan-N-Pick instructions. Students lead themselves through the thinking questions. For individual accountability, have each student record their own answer for each question.

2. Journal Writing Center

At a second center, have a Journal Writing activity page for each student. Students can discuss the question with others at their center, then write their own journal entry. After everyone is done writing, students share what they wrote with other students at their center.

3. Question Starters Center

At a third center, have a Question Starters page. Split the students at the center into two groups. Have both groups create thinking questions using the Question Starters activity page. When the groups are done writing their questions, they trade questions with the other group at their center. When done answering each other's questions, two groups pair up to compare their answers.

Caring and Empathy

higher-level thinking questions

Warm weather fosters growth: cold weather destroys it. Thus a man with an unsympathetic temperament has a scant joy: but a man with a warm and friendly heart overflowing blessings, and his beneficence will extend to posterity.

— Hung Tzu-Cheng

Higher-Level Thinking Questions for Character Development
Kagan Publishing • 1 (800) 933-2667 • www.KaganOnline.com

Caring and Empathy
Question Cards

Caring and Empathy

1 What is one act of kindness you have done for someone else that you are most proud of? Describe.

Caring and Empathy

2 Some people are very compassionate toward others. Some people don't care about (apathetic) others. Some people are down right mean toward others. What makes people treat others the way the do?

Caring and Empathy

3 Complete the following sentence. "Caring is…"

Caring and Empathy

4 John Donne, the English poet, wrote "No man is an island." What do you think he meant?

Caring and Empathy
Question Cards

Caring and Empathy

5 What are some things you do to show your friends you care?

Caring and Empathy

6 Can some people care for plants or animals the same way that others care for people?

Caring and Empathy

7 Describe a time in your life when someone really showed how much she or he cared about you. How did it make you feel?

Caring and Empathy

8 A Native American proverb says, "You can't understand another person until you walk a few miles in their moccasins." What does it mean to walk in someone else's shoes?

Higher-Level Thinking Questions for Character Development
Kagan Publishing • 1 (800) 933-2667 • www.KaganOnline.com

Caring and Empathy
Question Cards

Caring and Empathy

9 Ann Landers said, "Hate is like acid. It can damage the vessel in which it is stored as well as destroy the object on which it is poured." Complete the following metaphor: "Love is like…"

Caring and Empathy

10 The more you give, the more you receive. Do you think this is possible? If so, how?

Caring and Empathy

11 Mother Teresa spent much of her life loving needy people. She said, "I have found the paradox that if I love until it hurts, then there is no hurt, but only more love." What does it mean to love until it hurts?

Caring and Empathy

12 People show they care in different ways. Some do things for others. Some say nice things. Some give gifts. Some have positive thoughts. In your opinion, what are the best ways to show you care?

Caring and Empathy
Question Cards

Caring and Empathy

13 If you were a parent and wanted to teach your daughter about the importance of seeing things through someone else's eyes, what would you do or say?

Caring and Empathy

14 A new girl in your class is from a faraway country. She doesn't speak your language very well, and dresses differently from everyone else. How does she feel? What could you do for her?

Caring and Empathy

15 A student in your school was born without legs. He rides in a wheelchair. A lot of kids think he is weird and won't talk to him. How do you think he feels? What do you do?

Caring and Empathy

16 Who in your life do you most care for? What makes you care for them more than for others?

Higher-Level Thinking Questions for Character Development
Kagan Publishing • 1 (800) 933-2667 • www.KaganOnline.com

Caring and Empathy
Journal Writing Question

Write your response to the question below.
Be ready to share your response.

John Donne, the English poet, wrote "No man is an island." What do you think he meant?

_____
_____
_____
_____
_____
_____
_____
_____
_____
_____
_____
_____
_____
_____
_____
_____
_____
_____
_____
_____
_____

Caring and Empathy
Question Starters

Use the question starters below to create complete questions.
Send your questions to a partner or to another team to answer.

1. Why is it important

2. If no one cared

3. How would you feel if

4. When in your life

5. Why do people

6. How would you rate

7. Why should we

8. Do other people

Higher-Level Thinking Questions for Character Development
Kagan Publishing • 1 (800) 933-2667 • www.KaganOnline.com

Character
Questions

higher-level thinking questions

During my eighty-seven years, I have witnessed a whole succession of technological revolutions. But none of them has done away with the need for character in the individual or the ability to think.

— Bernard M. Baruch

Higher-Level Thinking Questions for Character Development
Kagan Publishing • 1 (800) 933-2667 • www.KaganOnline.com

Character Questions
Question Cards

Character Questions

1 Who is your hero? What traits or qualities does he or she have that you admire most?

Character Questions

2 How would you define the word "character"?

Character Questions

3 What character trait do you value most? Why?

Character Questions

4 Describe a book you've read that has a message about the importance of character.

Character Questions
Question Cards

5 Think of a movie you've recently seen. Is the lead role a person of high or low character? Give examples to support your claim.

6 What does the following quote mean: "Stand for what's right, even when you stand alone"?

7 Is morals the same thing as values?

8 Character is who you are and what you do when no one else is looking. Do you agree with this quote? Why or why not?

Higher-Level Thinking Questions for Character Development
Kagan Publishing • 1 (800) 933-2667 • www.KaganOnline.com

Character Questions
Question Cards

9 Martin Luther King, Jr., the famous civil rights activist said, "I look to a day when people will not be judged by the color of their skin, but by the content of their character." Why should we judge others by the content of their characters rather than by how they look?

10 There are absolute rights and wrongs that every person should know about. Do you agree or disagree?

11 What are the advantages of living a life of positive character?

12 Describe a person lacking character.

Character Questions
Question Cards

Character Questions

13 What general statement can you make about character?

Character Questions

14 On a scale of 1 to 10, how would your best friend rate your character? Describe his or her rating.

Character Questions

15 What events and experiences in your life have shaped your character? Give specific examples.

Character Questions

16 Which character traits would you most like to improve? How could you improve it?

Higher-Level Thinking Questions for Character Development
Kagan Publishing • 1 (800) 933-2667 • www.KaganOnline.com

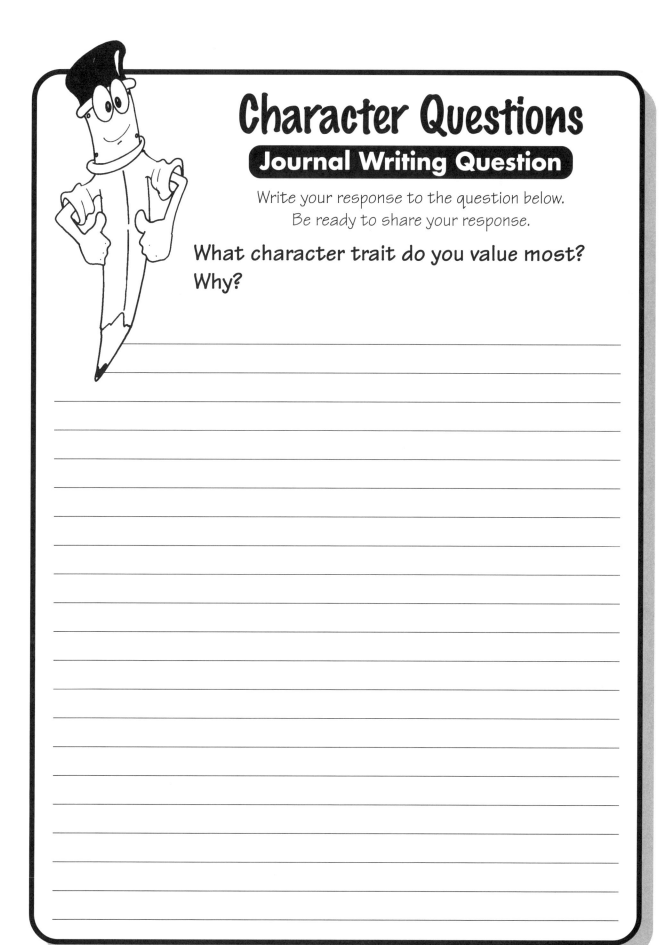

Character Questions
Journal Writing Question

Write your response to the question below.
Be ready to share your response.

What character trait do you value most? Why?

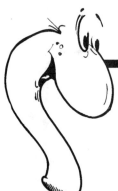

Character Questions
Question Starters

Use the question starters below to create complete questions.
Send your questions to a partner or to another team to answer.

1. How would you describe

2. What role does

3. Does character

4. How do you feel about

5. How honest

6. Is integrity

 7. How do you decide

8. Who do you

Higher-Level Thinking Questions for Character Development
Kagan Publishing • 1 (800) 933-2667 • www.KaganOnline.com

Character
Quotations

higher-level thinking questions

He that has light within his own clear breast may sit in the center, and enjoy bright day: But he that hides a dark soul and foul thoughts benighted walks under the midday sun.

— John Milton

Character Quotations
Question Cards

Character Quotations

1 "Our character is what we do when we think no one is looking."
— H. Jackson Browne

Why do people act differently in public than when they're alone?

Character Quotations

2 "The ultimate measure of a man is not where he stands in moments of comfort, but where he stands at times of challenge and controversy."
— Martin Luther King, Jr.

Why might Dr. King think difficult situations are a true test of a person's character?

Character Quotations

3 "Many a man's reputation would not know his character if they met on the street."
— Elbert Hubbard

What is the difference between character and reputation?

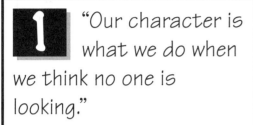

Character Quotations

4 "Nearly all men can stand adversity, but if you want to test a man's character, give him power."
— Abraham Lincoln

How is power a test of a person's character?

Character Quotations
Question Cards

Character Quotations

5 "Character cannot be developed in ease and quiet. Only through experience of trial and suffering can the soul be strengthened, ambition inspired, and success achieved."
— Helen Keller
How does experience shape a person's character?

Character Quotations

6 "When you choose your friends, don't be short-changed by choosing personality over character."
— W. Somerset Maugham
What is the difference between someone's personality and their character? How do you choose your friends?

Character Quotations

7 "The true test of character is not how much we know how to do, but how we behave when we don't know what to do."
— John Holt
What are situations which test our character?

Character Quotations

8 "Always do right — this will gratify some and astonish the rest."
— Mark Twain
What is the meaning of this quotation?

Higher-Level Thinking Questions for Character Development
Kagan Publishing • 1 (800) 933-2667 • www.KaganOnline.com

Character Quotations
Question Cards

Character Quotations

9 "Of all the properties which belong to honorable men, not one is so highly prized as that of character."
— Henry Clay
Do you consider your character to be your most prized possession? Why or why not?

Character Quotations

10 "Die when I may, I want it said by those who knew me best that I always plucked a thistle and planted a flower where I thought a flower would grow."
— Abraham Lincoln
What did President Lincoln mean by this? What does it say about his character?

Character Quotations

11 "The final forming of a person's character lies in their own hands."
— Anne Frank
Why is your character ultimately your own responsibility? Explain.

Character Quotations

12 "Who you are speaks so loudly I can't hear what you're saying."
— Ralph Waldo Emerson
What does this quotation say about character?

Character Quotations
Question Cards

Character Quotations

13 "That which does not kill us will only make us stronger."
— Unknown

How can we use difficult situations to strengthen our character?

Character Quotations

14 "Education has for its object the formation of character."
— Herbert Spencer

How do schools try to build students' characters? Are they successful?

Character Quotations

15 "The time is always right to do what is right."
— Martin Luther King, Jr.

In your opinion, what is "Right" and what is "Wrong"?

Character Quotations

16 "Let us endeavor so to live that when we come to die even the undertaker will be sorry."
— Mark Twain

What kind of life would a person have to live so that even the undertaker would be sorry?

Higher-Level Thinking Questions for Character Development
Kagan Publishing • 1 (800) 933-2667 • www.KaganOnline.com

Character Quotations

Journal Writing Question

Write your response to the question below.
Be ready to share your response.

"Of all the properties which belong to honorable men, not one is so highly prized as that of character."

— Henry Clay

Do you consider your character to be your most prized possession? Why or why not?

_____

_____

_____

_____

_____

_____

_____

_____

_____

_____

_____

_____

_____

_____

_____

_____

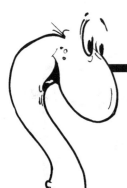

Character Quotations

Question Starters

Use the question starters below to create complete questions.
Send your questions to a partner or to another team to answer.

1. What would you do if _____

_____

2. What role does character _____

_____

3. What situations _____

_____

4. How would you decide what to do if _____

_____

5. What grade would you give _____

_____

6. How could you improve _____

_____

7. How would you feel if _____

_____

8. In your life _____

_____

Higher-Level Thinking Questions for Character Development
Kagan Publishing • 1 (800) 933-2667 • www.KaganOnline.com

Citizenship

higher-level thinking questions

"There can be no daily democracy without daily citizenship.

— Ralph Nader

Higher-Level Thinking Questions for Character Development
Kagan Publishing • 1 (800) 933-2667 • www.KaganOnline.com

Citizenship
Question Cards

Citizenship

1 On a scale of 1 to 100, how would you rate your citizenship skills? Explain why you rated yourself as you did.

Citizenship

2 What are the traits of a good citizen?

Citizenship

3 Should burning the flag be against the law? If so why, and what should the penalty be? If not, why not?

Citizenship

4 You become very good friends with a foreign exchange student of the opposite sex. Because she or he is not a U.S. citizen, she or he must leave the country at the end of the school year. Would you marry him or her so he or she could become a U.S. citizen? Why or why not?

Citizenship
Question Cards

Citizenship

5 If you were old enough to vote in the presidential elections, would you vote? Why do you think there are so many people who are eligible to vote that don't cast their ballot? How could our country increase voting?

Citizenship

6 As a citizen of this country, what rights do you have? What responsibilities do you have?

Citizenship

7 What would you consider a bad citizen?

Citizenship

8 You come out of your grocery store and a nice lady asks you to sign her petition. You ask her what it's for and she tells you it is to stop the development of a nearby shopping complex that will have a movie theater and restaurants. She says it will cause too much tourism and traffic. You like the idea of a nearby movie theater, but don't care for more traffic. What do you do?

Higher-Level Thinking Questions for Character Development
Kagan Publishing • 1 (800) 933-2667 • www.KaganOnline.com

Citizenship
Question Cards

Citizenship

9 Rosa Parks has been honored for breaking an unjust law. Is it ever right to break the law?

Citizenship

10 You are a judge. A teenager is given a ticket for skateboarding in the parking lot of the bank. He is in your court to fight the ticket. He is clearly in violation of the city code. However, you feel teenagers should have the right to skateboard where they please as long as they are not endangering themselves or others. What do you do?

Citizenship

11 Your teacher puts you in small groups for a project. Your project is to somehow serve your community in a positive way. Give ideas how your group might serve the community.

Citizenship

12 Are you being a bad citizen if you speak out against acts of the government you don't believe in?

Citizenship
Question Cards

Citizenship

13 Another country is having a civil war over whether to have a democracy or communist form of government. Your country sides with the democratic side of the country and sends in military troops to help fight the war. You feel it is their war, and none of our business. You are drafted to go fight. What do you do?

Citizenship

14 Your next door neighbor has a black box and is getting free cable TV. If you turn him in, are you being a good citizen? Why or why not?

Citizenship

15 In your community, there is a historical building that belongs to the city. It is being used as a restaurant. You are the chairperson of the board that decides what to do with the building. You and the board favor using the building as a cultural center. If the board votes, the cultural center wins. If the city votes, the restaurant may stay. What do you do?

Citizenship

16 To be a good citizen, you must be born in the country. Do you agree or disagree? Explain your position.

Higher-Level Thinking Questions for Character Development
Kagan Publishing • 1 (800) 933-2667 • www.KaganOnline.com

Citizenship
Journal Writing Question

Write your response to the question below.
Be ready to share your response.

As a citizen of this country, what rights do you have? What responsibilities do you have?

_____

_____

_____

_____

_____

_____

_____

_____

_____

_____

_____

_____

_____

_____

_____

_____

_____

_____

_____

Citizenship

Question Starters

Use the question starters below to create complete questions.
Send your questions to a partner or to another team to answer.

1. Should all citizens

2. What is the importance of

3. How could you improve

4. What is your opinion about

5. What would you do if

6. Who do you consider

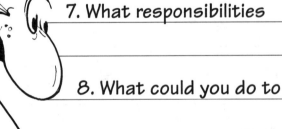

7. What responsibilities

8. What could you do to

58

Conflict
Resolution and
Peacemaking

higher-level thinking questions

"Preventing conflicts is the work of politics; establishing peace is the work of education.

— Maria Montessori

Higher-Level Thinking Questions for Character Development
Kagan Publishing • 1 (800) 933-2667 • www.KaganOnline.com

Conflict Resolution and Peacemaking
Question Cards

Conflict Resolution and Peacemaking

1 What is the biggest conflict you've ever been in? How was it resolved? Would you do anything differently if you were in the same situation again?

Conflict Resolution and Peacemaking

2 What are some reasons conflicts occur between people?

Conflict Resolution and Peacemaking

3 Do you think there will ever be a time when there are no more wars? Why or why not?

Conflict Resolution and Peacemaking

4 You are baby-sitting two brothers. They both want to play with the same toy truck. They start to fight over the truck. What do you do?

Conflict Resolution and Peacemaking
Question Cards

5 You are the chief of police in a big city. Two of your officers are being tried in court for police brutality. They were caught on tape beating an African American. If your policemen are found not guilty, you fear there may be race riots. What do you do?

6 Pretend you are a mother. Your two daughters are always in competition for your attention. They try to outdo each other. It hurts you to see them competing against each other for your love. What do you do?

7 There are lots of ways conflicts can be resolved such as: sharing, taking turns, using humor, compromising, using chance, getting outside help, postponing. Which method do you think is best for resolving conflicts? Explain.

8 You are the president. There are two different religious groups that are fighting with each other. They both want to live on the same land and don't want the other group to live there. What would you do?

Higher-Level Thinking Questions for Character Development
Kagan Publishing • 1 (800) 933-2667 • www.KaganOnline.com

Conflict Resolution and Peacemaking
Question Cards

Conflict Resolution and Peacemaking

9 You are trying to read your book. A classmate of yours is tapping her pencil on the desk and bothering you. You politely ask her to stop, but she says, "Sorry, it helps me concentrate." What do you do?

Conflict Resolution and Peacemaking

10 Thomas Jefferson, the celebrated U.S. statesman, once said, "When angry, count to ten before you speak; if very angry, a hundred." Why would he suggest counting before speaking?

Conflict Resolution and Peacemaking

11 You are standing in a long line to buy lunch. Someone takes cuts in front of you to wait in line with a friend. You don't think that's fair. You want to let the person know, but don't want to start a fight. What can you do?

Conflict Resolution and Peacemaking

12 Nelson Mandela, the South African leader in the nonapartheid movement, said, "If you want to make peace with your enemy, you have to work with your enemy. Then he becomes your partner."

Conflict Resolution and Peacemaking
Question Cards

Conflict Resolution and Peacemaking

13 Why are conflict resolution skills good skills for people to have?

Conflict Resolution and Peacemaking

14 How can communication work to solve a conflict? How can communication make the situation worse?

Conflict Resolution and Peacemaking

15 Racism, prejudice, discrimination, and lack of respect are all causes of conflict. These types of conflicts could be avoided if people were more tolerant of others and respectful of diversity. How might people learn to appreciate diversity?

Conflict Resolution and Peacemaking

16 Do you think people have a natural tendency to be aggressive and violent, or is it something they learn by example? Explain.

Higher-Level Thinking Questions for Character Development
Kagan Publishing • 1 (800) 933-2667 • www.KaganOnline.com

Conflict Resolution and Peacemaking

Journal Writing Question

Write your response to the question below.
Be ready to share your response.

How can communication work to solve a conflict? How can communication make the situation worse?

_____
_____
_____
_____
_____
_____
_____
_____
_____
_____
_____
_____
_____
_____
_____
_____
_____
_____
_____
_____
_____

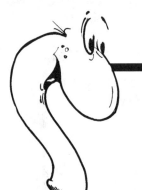

Conflict Resolution and Peacemaking

Question Starters

Use the question starters below to create complete questions.
Send your questions to a partner or to another team to answer.

1. When in your life

2. If the world was at peace

3. What conflicts

4. How would you rate

5. Why *do* people

6. What solutions

7. What skills

8. Who needs

Higher-Level Thinking Questions for Character Development
Kagan Publishing • 1 (800) 933-2667 • www.KaganOnline.com

Courage

higher-level thinking questions

"We must build dikes of courage to hold back the flood of fear."

— Martin Luther King, Jr.

Higher-Level Thinking Questions for Character Development
Kagan Publishing • 1 (800) 933-2667 • www.KaganOnline.com

Courage
Question Cards

1 Is courage the same thing as fearlessness? Why or why not?

2 What is the bravest thing you've ever done? Why do you consider it so brave?

3 When you are bucked off a horse, it takes a lot of courage to get back in the saddle. What horses have you been bucked off of in your life? Did you get back in the saddle?

4 Your school's windows get broken. One of the kids who did it brags about it to you. You fear if you tell, you may be harmed. What do you do?

Courage
Question Cards

Courage

5 You strongly believe nuclear weapon testing should be banned. A group of people are going to protest a testing. You know you may go to jail if you protest. Would you protest? Why or why not?

Courage

6 Integrity is being true to your values. Why does it sometimes take courage to have integrity?

Courage

7 Complete the following analogy. "As courageous as…" Explain your analogy.

Courage

8 Franklin D. Roosevelt was a U.S. president during a difficult time in the country's history. He said, "There is nothing to fear but fear itself." What did he mean?

Higher-Level Thinking Questions for Character Development
Kagan Publishing • 1 (800) 933-2667 • www.KaganOnline.com

Courage
Question Cards

Courage

9 What is your greatest fear? Why does it scare you so much? How could you face your fear? Would you be less afraid?

Courage

10 Your class is putting on a play. You are perfect for the main character. The only problem is that the idea of acting in front of an audience gives you butterflies in your stomach. Do you face your fear to act in the play?

Courage

11 To be brave, sometimes we have to put aside our fear. Why do you think we have fears?

Courage

12 Who is the most courageous person you know? What makes him or her so courageous?

Courage

13 "Life shrinks or expands in proportion to one's courage."
— Anaïs Nin
What does this quotation mean?

Courage

14 In another faraway country some evil dictator is killing innocent people because they are a different race. Your country is going to go to war to stop the killing. Would you have the courage to risk your life for this cause?

Courage

15 When in your life were you most scared? Explain. Were you or someone else courageous in the situation?

Courage

16 What scares you more: an accident, losing a loved one, death, giving a speech, blood, natural disaster, war, being embarrassed, growing up, bullies, the dark, or something else? Explain why.

Higher-Level Thinking Questions for Character Development
Kagan Publishing • 1 (800) 933-2667 • www.KaganOnline.com

Courage

Journal Writing Question

Write your response to the question below.
Be ready to share your response.

What is your greatest fear? Why does it scare you so much? How could you face your fear? Would you be less afraid?

_____
_____
_____
_____
_____
_____
_____
_____
_____
_____
_____
_____
_____
_____
_____
_____
_____
_____
_____
_____
_____
_____

Courage

Question Starters

Use the question starters below to create complete questions.
Send your questions to a partner or to another team to answer.

1. How is fear _____

_____

2. Why is courage _____

_____

3. What would give you the courage to _____

_____

4. How would you describe _____

_____

5. Would you be afraid _____

_____

6. What is the most courageous _____

_____

   7. How brave _____

_____

8. What would you do if _____

_____

Higher-Level Thinking Questions for Character Development
Kagan Publishing • 1 (800) 933-2667 • www.KaganOnline.com

Fairness, Justice, and Equality

higher-level thinking questions

"Nothing is to be preferred before justice.

— Socrates

Fairness, Justice, and Equality
Question Cards

1 Is life fair? Describe why or why not.

2 Three students in the class all want to use the class computer at the same time to work on different projects. What would be a fair solution?

3 At work, companies often have something called, "seniority." That means the longer you work for a company, the more priorities and advantages you get. Is seniority fair?

4 If someone kills someone else, what is a fair and just punishment?

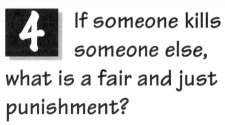

Fairness, Justice, and Equality
Question Cards

Fairness, Justice, and Equality

5 Women often make less money than a men for the same type of work. Obviously this is not fair. Why do you think it happens?

Fairness, Justice, and Equality

6 To be just, judges have to be impartial and fair. This means they should not have a bias. They must treat everyone equally. Would you make a good judge? What difficulties might a judge have?

Fairness, Justice, and Equality

7 The Declaration of Independence says, "all men are created equal." Do you think all people were created equal? Explain why or why not. Should everyone be treated equally?

Fairness, Justice, and Equality

8 Rich neighborhoods often have more money to spend on their schools than poor neighborhoods. Is this fair? What would be a fair solution?

Higher-Level Thinking Questions for Character Development
Kagan Publishing • 1 (800) 933-2667 • www.KaganOnline.com

Fairness, Justice, and Equality
Question Cards

Fairness, Justice, and Equality

9 Why did women and African Americans have to fight for years for their right to vote? Does our society treat everyone equally today?

Fairness, Justice, and Equality

10 Should the best teachers work with the students that need the most help, or should they work with the best and brightest students? What do you think is more fair? Explain you reasoning.

Fairness, Justice, and Equality

11 You are a juror on a murder trial. You really don't know if the defendant is innocent is guilty. Would you rather lock up an innocent person or let a murderer go free?

Fairness, Justice, and Equality

12 You wrote a report on the women's right to vote. Your teacher read it and said, "You really did this topic justice." What do you think she meant?

Fairness, Justice, and Equality
Question Cards

Fairness, Justice, and Equality

13 A drunk driver accidentally kills a mother and her child. Is there any difference between that and murder? What would be a fair punishment?

Fairness, Justice, and Equality

14 Affirmative action provides women and "minority" students advantages in getting into college and jobs because of the "disadvantages" they've encountered in their lives. Is affirmative action fair?

Fairness, Justice, and Equality

15 In school, we pledge to the flag every day. The pledge of allegiance for the U.S. ends with the phrase, "with liberty and justice for all." What does this mean to you?

Fairness, Justice, and Equality

16 An "eye for an eye" is a system of justice that says whatever bad thing you do to others should happen to you. Should we practice this type of justice?

Higher-Level Thinking Questions for Character Development
Kagan Publishing • 1 (800) 933-2667 • www.KaganOnline.com

Fairness, Justice, and Equality

Journal Writing Question

Write your response to the question below.
Be ready to share your response.

The Declaration of Independence says, "all men are created equal." Do you think all people were created equal? Explain why or why not. Should everyone be treated equally?

_____
_____
_____
_____
_____
_____
_____
_____
_____
_____
_____
_____
_____
_____
_____
_____
_____
_____

Fairness, Justice, and Equality

Question Starters

Use the question starters below to create complete questions.
Send your questions to a partner or to another team to answer.

1. What would be a fair solution for _____

_____

2. What inequalities _____

_____

3. When in your life _____

_____

4. If you were to rate _____

_____

5. Is it just that _____

_____

6. How would you feel if _____

_____

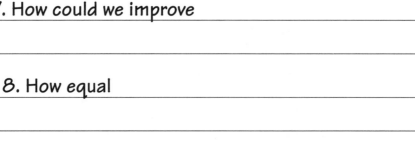

7. How could we improve _____

_____

8. How equal _____

_____

Higher-Level Thinking Questions for Character Development
Kagan Publishing • 1 (800) 933-2667 • www.KaganOnline.com

Honesty

higher-level thinking questions

"The naked truth is always better than the best-dressed lie.

— Ann Landers

Higher-Level Thinking Questions for Character Development
Kagan Publishing • 1 (800) 933-2667 • www.KaganOnline.com

Honesty
Question Cards

Honesty

1 Your grandma knits you a sweater for Christmas. You open your gift and think the sweater is ugly and outdated. Do you say you like it to spare her feelings or do you tell her the truth?

Honesty

2 Benjamin Franklin said, "Half the truth is often a great lie." What do you think he meant?

Honesty

3 Your next door neighbor is a little boy. He lost a tooth and got a dollar under his pillow for it. He asks you if there is really such a thing as the Tooth Fairy. Do you lie to him? What do you say?

Honesty

4 You are the president of the United States. You think a war with another country is a possibility. However, you do not want to announce your plans to the public because you fear the other country may find out. Are you lying to the public? Is this okay? Why or why not?

Honesty
Question Cards

Honesty

5 Your dad got a haircut and it looks terrible on him. He's happy about his haircut. He smiles at you and asks, "How does it look?" How do you respond? Why?

Honesty

6 You have a bicycle that you want to sell. You put an ad in the newspaper and a stranger comes to your house to look at it. She asks, "Is there anything wrong with the bike?" The frame has a small crack in it, but she didn't notice. Do you tell her about the crack even if it means she may not buy the bike? Why or why not?

Honesty

7 George Washington said. "Honesty is the best policy." Do you agree? Why or why not?

Honesty

8 You are a surgeon in the emergency room. A man is brought in that was hit by a bus. You don't think you will be able to save him. He asks you, "Doc, tell me the truth, Am I going to make it?" What do you say?

Higher-Level Thinking Questions for Character Development
Kagan Publishing • 1 (800) 933-2667 • www.KaganOnline.com

Honesty
Question Cards

Honesty

9 Is lying bad? Always? Sometimes? Explain.

Honesty

10 You work in the advertising department of a vitamin company. Your boss writes an ad and asks you to design the graphics. After reading the ad, you know what he wrote will mislead buyers. Do you tell him you think the ad is dishonest, or do you do what he tells you?

Honesty

11 You are the owner of a small clothing store. It is the Fourth of July. Your store is open until 9 P.M., but you get off at noon. You plan to have a picnic with your family at the beach. At noon, your employee calls in to say she is feeling sick and can't work. You think she may be lying to get the night off to have fun. What do you do?

Honesty

12 You are riding your skateboard in a business park that does not permit skateboarding. As you are exiting the business park, the security officer stops you. He asks you, were you riding your skateboard in there? What do you say?

Honesty
Question Cards

Honesty

13 On a scale of 1 to 10, how would you rate your own honesty? Explain your rating.

Honesty

14 Imagine there was a lying alarm. It was a bracelet that flashed and made buzzing sounds when someone told a lie. If such an alarm existed would you vote to require everyone to wear one? Why or why not?

Honesty

15 You see your sister going through your mom's wallet. Later, your mom comes up to you and looks very disappointed. She asks you, "Did you take money out of my wallet?" Do you tell her you saw your sister going through her wallet?

Honesty

16 What positive benefits come from telling the truth? For the truthteller? For others?

Higher-Level Thinking Questions for Character Development
Kagan Publishing • 1 (800) 933-2667 • www.KaganOnline.com

Honesty

Journal Writing Question

Write your response to the question below.
Be ready to share your response.

George Washington said. "Honesty is the best policy." Do you agree? Why or why not?

_____
_____
_____
_____
_____
_____
_____
_____
_____
_____
_____
_____
_____
_____
_____
_____
_____
_____
_____

Honesty

Question Starters

Use the question starters below to create complete questions.
Send your questions to a partner or to another team to answer.

1. If you lied

_____

2. Have you ever

_____

3. What's more important

_____

4. Would you tell the truth if

_____

5. How would you feel if

_____

6. Why might

_____

7. What would you think if

_____

8. How honest

_____

Higher-Level Thinking Questions for Character Development
Kagan Publishing • 1 (800) 933-2667 • www.KaganOnline.com

Integrity

higher-level thinking questions

"One must not conceal any part of what one has recognized to be true.

— Albert Einstein

Higher-Level Thinking Questions for Character Development
Kagan Publishing • 1 (800) 933-2667 • www.KaganOnline.com

Integrity
Question Cards

Integrity

1 To have integrity, you must be true to what you believe. What do you believe in? Use the following sentence to describe three things you believe in: "I believe in _____ because..."

Integrity

2 You are with your friend listening to a new CD. Your friend says, "This CD rocks. What do you think of it?" You really don't like it, but say it's cool. Deep down inside, you know you don't like it. Is that acting with integrity? Why or why not? What is the difference between integrity and honesty?

Integrity

3 When we do something we know is wrong, we are acting without integrity. Describe one time you acted without integrity. What would have been the right thing to do?

Integrity

4 You are lawyer. A client comes in and says, he would like to sue a company because he fell down the stairs in front of their building. The company will probably give him money to avoid going to court. You will make money too. But you don't think the company should be held responsible. Do you represent the client? Why or why not?

Integrity

5 You are in the toy store and really want to buy a special gift for your brother. You don't have the money to buy it and know it's not right to steal. But you know you can put it in your pocket and no one would know. Do you steal it?

Integrity

6 You get your report on the rain forest back from your teacher. In your report, you argue that it should be illegal to take pets from the rain forest. Your teacher has a parrot as a pet and disagrees. She says you can get a D or write a new report. What do you do?

Integrity

7 What does it mean to practice what you preach? Do you? Give one specific example.

Integrity

8 You think killing is a terrible thing and anyone who kills someone else should be locked up for the rest of their life. You find out your favorite uncle killed someone. Do you think he should be locked up for life even though you love him?

Higher-Level Thinking Questions for Character Development
Kagan Publishing • 1 (800) 933-2667 • www.KaganOnline.com

Integrity
Question Cards

Integrity

9 Peer pressure is when your friends push you into something you don't think is right. Have you ever done something you didn't feel good about because you felt pressured to do it?

Integrity

10 Are there ever situations where it is best to act against your own values? Explain.

Integrity

11 Integrity is living up to your own moral standards. You know someone who lies, cheats and steals but doesn't have a problem behaving that way. Does he or she have integrity? Why or why not?

Integrity

12 Your friends think it would be cool to spray paint the school's playground. You think it is vandalism. If you don't join your friends, they may not like you as much. What do you do?

Integrity
Question Cards

Integrity

13 If you disagreed with a law, would you violate the law? Why or why not?

Integrity

14 You think cheating is bad and people should work hard to earn their grades. The cutest guy or girl in the class is sitting next to you and is looking at your paper. Would you let him or her cheat off you? Why or why not?

Integrity

15 Rude drivers really make you mad. You think people should be more polite to each other. Your friend's dad is driving you home from the movies. A car accidentally cuts him off and your friend's dad starts honking, and yelling at the guy. When you get home, your friend says, "That was cool, huh?" What do you say?

Integrity

16 Integrity is acting consistently with your beliefs and values. How do you know your own beliefs and values?

Higher-Level Thinking Questions for Character Development
Kagan Publishing • 1 (800) 933-2667 • www.KaganOnline.com

Integrity

Journal Writing Question

Write your response to the question below.
Be ready to share your response.

When we do something we know is wrong, we are acting without integrity. Describe one time you acted without integrity. What would have been the right thing to do?

_____
_____
_____
_____
_____
_____
_____
_____
_____
_____
_____
_____
_____
_____
_____
_____
_____

Integrity

Question Starters

Use the question starters below to create complete questions.
Send your questions to a partner or to another team to answer.

1. Do you believe

2. Who do you know

3. Have you ever

4. What would you do if

5. What values

6. Do your actions

7. What could you say if

8. What might happen if

Higher-Level Thinking Questions for Character Development
Kagan Publishing • 1 (800) 933-2667 • www.KaganOnline.com

Leadership

higher-level thinking questions

"The wicked leader is he who the people despise. The good leader is he who the people revere. The great leader is he who the people say, we did it ourselves.

— Lao-Tzu

Higher-Level Thinking Questions for Character Development
Kagan Publishing • 1 (800) 933-2667 • www.KaganOnline.com

Leadership
Question Cards

Leadership

1 What are five qualities of a good leader? Describe why each is a good quality.

Leadership

2 You are the manager in a store and just hired a new employee. She keeps getting too many personal phone calls at work. What do you do?

Leadership

3 What are three jobs that require leadership skills? Describe the leadership skills involved in each job.

Leadership

4 Are you more of a leader or more of a follower? Explain.

Leadership
Question Cards

5 Do you think the president is a good leader? Why or why not?

6 When in your life will you have to be a leader? How do you feel about that leadership role?

7 You are working on a team project. There is someone on your team who is not participating. What can you do to include him or her?

8 What responsibilities does a leader have?

Higher-Level Thinking Questions for Character Development
Kagan Publishing • 1 (800) 933-2667 • www.KaganOnline.com

Leadership
Question Cards

Leadership

9 The leader should always be the smartest person in the group. Do you agree or disagree?

Leadership

10 Describe one time in your life when you were a leader. Why were you the leader? Who did you lead? What did you think of being the leader?

Leadership

11 Who do you think is the best leader of all time? Why?

Leadership

12 If we had no leaders, do you think the world would be a better or a worse place? Describe your thinking.

Leadership
Question Cards

Leadership

13 Some leaders tell everyone what to do. Some leaders want people to lead themselves. Which leadership style is more effective? Why?

Leadership

14 Public speaking is an important leadership skill. However, on some surveys, people fear speaking in public even more than death. Why is it so scary for so many people?

Leadership

15 What *do you* think is the most important leadership skill? Why is it such an important skill?

Leadership

16 What steps could you take to work on your leadership skills?

Higher-Level Thinking Questions for Character Development
Kagan Publishing • 1 (800) 933-2667 • www.KaganOnline.com

Leadership

Journal Writing Question

Write your response to the question below.
Be ready to share your response.

Are you more of a leader or more of a
follower? Explain your answer.

_____

_____

_____

_____

_____

_____

_____

_____

_____

_____

_____

_____

_____

_____

_____

_____

_____

_____

Leadership

Question Starters

Use the question starters below to create complete questions.
Send your questions to a partner or to another team to answer.

1. Why do people

2. Which leader

3. What would you do if

4. What characteristics

5. If you were elected

6. How would you

7. How does a good leader

8. In your life

Higher-Level Thinking Questions for Character Development
Kagan Publishing • 1 (800) 933-2667 • www.KaganOnline.com

Loyalty

higher-level thinking questions

"Loyalty is still the same, whether it win or lose the game; true as a dial to the sun, although it be not shined upon.

— Samuel Butler

Loyalty
Question Cards

Loyalty

1 How is a loyal person different from a disloyal person? Contrast the two types of people.

Loyalty

2 Do you consider yourself loyal to someone or something? Explain.

Loyalty

3 Are there ever times when you should not be loyal?

Loyalty

4 You are in the watch store in the mall. Your friend slips a watch into your pocket. He asks you to be a loyal friend and steal it for him. What do you do?

Loyalty
Question Cards

Loyalty

5 If you were going to write a song about loyalty, what ideas would you want to include in your song?

Loyalty

6 You work for a used car sales company. You feel loyal to your boss and your job. You get a car on your lot with engine problems. Your boss wants you to sell it, but not tell the buyers. Do you remain loyal to your boss? Why or why not?

Loyalty

7 Rank your loyalty to: your family, your friends, your beliefs, your country. Who are you most loyal to? Who are you least loyal to? Why?

Loyalty

8 "Brand loyalty" is being loyal to a brand or product. Are you loyal to any brand or product? If so, describe why? If not, why might people be loyal to brands?

Higher-Level Thinking Questions for Character Development
Kagan Publishing • 1 (800) 933-2667 • www.KaganOnline.com

Loyalty
Question Cards

9 To be completely loyal may be to do something you don't believe in. What is more important to you personally, loyalty or integrity?

10 Is anyone loyal to you? If so, who and in which way? If not, why not?

11 "Loyal like a dog" is a common expression. In what ways are dogs loyal? What animal would you use in the expression: "Unloyal like a _____?" Why?

12 Complete the following sentence. "Loyalty is..."

Loyalty
Question Cards

Loyalty

13 How would the world be different if no one was loyal to anyone but themselves?

Loyalty

14 Pick the main character from your favorite movie. Is he or she a loyal person? Use specific examples from the movie to support your position.

Loyalty

15 Your country goes to war. It is a war you don't believe in. You are drafted to fight in the war. Do you remain loyal to your country?

Loyalty

16 If your parents committed a serious crime, would you remain loyal to them? Why or why not?

Higher-Level Thinking Questions for Character Development
Kagan Publishing • 1 (800) 933-2667 • www.KaganOnline.com

Loyalty

Journal Writing Question

Write your response to the question below.
Be ready to share your response.

Are there ever times when you should not be loyal?

_____
_____
_____
_____
_____
_____
_____
_____
_____
_____
_____
_____
_____
_____
_____
_____
_____
_____
_____
_____
_____

Loyalty

Question Starters

Use the question starters below to create complete questions.
Send your questions to a partner or to another team to answer.

1. How would you feel if

2. What problems

3. What general rule

4. If no one was loyal

5. How would you evaluate

6. If you were really loyal

7. What situation

8. What would you do if

Higher-Level Thinking Questions for Character Development
Kagan Publishing • 1 (800) 933-2667 • www.KaganOnline.com

Patience

higher-level thinking questions

If I have made any valuable discoveries, it has been owing more to patient attention than to any other talent.

— Sir Isaac Newton

Higher-Level Thinking Questions for Character Development
Kagan Publishing • 1 (800) 933-2667 • www.KaganOnline.com

Patience
Question Cards

Patience

1 Do you consider yourself a patient person? Why or why not? Give specific examples.

Patience

2 Describe one time when you really lost your patience. Why were you impatient? How could you be more patient?

Patience

3 You and your friend are building a model. Your friend is building a small part but taking forever. You want to finish so you can paint the model. What do you do or say?

Patience

4 Why is patience an important virtue?

Patience
Question Cards

Patience

5 How is impatience like frustration? How is it different?

Patience

6 Your friends come over to your house to play. Your mom says you can't go outside until you finish your homework. You tell your friends to wait for you, you'll be out in a minute. Ten minutes later you figure you'll need at least another twenty minutes. Your friends are getting impatient. What do you do or say?

Patience

7 Describe one situation when you were very patient. How were you so patient? How did it make you feel?

Patience

8 Pretend you are a parent. Your daughter is in a school play and you take your younger son to watch her play. Your son is getting antsy and keeps saying, "I want to go...I want to go!" What do you do or say?

Patience
Question Cards

9 Imagine everyone in the world was impatient. How would the world be different?

10 People who are impatient are just selfish. Do you agree or disagree with this statement?

11 Pretend you are a server at a fancy restaurant. You are very busy, covering more tables than you can handle. A lady asked you for an iced tea. You have ten other requests in front of her. In a mean voice she says, "Excuse me...I've been waiting forever!" What do you do or say?

12 Someone is very impatient with you. They are getting irritated with you because you are taking a long time. How do they make you feel?

Patience
Question Cards

Patience

13 You are with your grandmother in the store. Her cart is blocking the aisle. A man comes into the aisle with his cart, waits for a few seconds, then blurts out, "Come on, move your cart old lady." How does it make you feel? What do you do?

Patience

14 Who is the most patient person you have ever met? How did you feel about him or her?

Patience

15 Abraham Lincoln said, "Things may come to those who wait, but only the things left by those who hustle." What does this say about patience?

Patience

16 How would you define patience?

Higher-Level Thinking Questions for Character Development
Kagan Publishing • 1 (800) 933-2667 • www.KaganOnline.com

Patience

Journal Writing Question

Write your response to the question below.
Be ready to share your response.

Do you consider yourself a patient person? Why or why not? Give specific examples.

_____

_____

_____

_____

_____

_____

_____

_____

_____

_____

_____

_____

_____

_____

_____

_____

_____

_____

_____

Patience

Question Starters

Use the question starters below to create complete questions.
Send your questions to a partner or to another team to answer.

1. When in your life

2. How do you feel about

3. If you wanted to be more patient

4. Why is patience

5. Have you ever

6. What advantages

7. How would you describe

8. When might

Higher-Level Thinking Questions for Character Development
Kagan Publishing • 1 (800) 933-2667 • www.KaganOnline.com

Perseverance

higher-level thinking questions

"Never, never, never, never give up."

— Winston Churchill

Higher-Level Thinking Questions for Character Development
Kagan Publishing • 1 (800) 933-2667 • www.KaganOnline.com

Perseverance
Question Cards

Perseverance

1 Who is the most successful person you know? What role did perseverance play in his or her success?

Perseverance

2 Thomas Edison, probably the most famous inventor of all time, once said "Genius is one percent inspiration and 99 percent perspiration." What does this say about perseverance?

Perseverance

3 Think about these two proverbs: 1) "If at first you don't succeed, try and try again." 2) "Don't beat a dead horse." What do they mean? Can they both be right? Why or why not?

Perseverance

4 Perseverance is a virtue. But are there times it is a mistake to persevere?

Perseverance
Question Cards

Perseverance

5 What is one thing you have accomplished in your life that you are most proud of? How would you feel now if you gave up before you accomplished your goal?

Perseverance

6 "Rome was not built in a day." What does this common saying say about the importance of perseverance?

Perseverance

7 You have a friend or acquaintance that can't seem to win. She never seems to succeed. She is feeling blue. What can you say to motivate her to not give up?

Perseverance

8 How can failure be a positive experience?

Higher-Level Thinking Questions for Character Development
Kagan Publishing • 1 (800) 933-2667 • www.KaganOnline.com

Perseverance
Question Cards

Perseverance

9 If you are trying to accomplish a goal and feel like giving up, what are some things you can tell yourself to persevere?

Perseverance

10 Thomas J. Watson said, "Go ahead and make mistakes. Make all you can. Because remember, that's where you'll find success." How might we find success in our mistakes?

Perseverance

11 Has anything really bad ever happened to you or to someone close to you? How did you or that person cope with the situation?

Perseverance

12 When in your life have you just given up? How do you feel about giving up?

Perseverance
Question Cards

Perseverance

13 Thomas Jefferson, one of the founding fathers of the U.S., once said, "I find that the harder I work, the more luck I seem to have." Why might we get luckier when we work hard?

Perseverance

14 Some people believe the harder the task, the sweeter the success. Do you feel better about your success if it comes to you easily or if it comes to you after working long and hard? Describe why.

Perseverance

15 Pretend you have a daughter. She really wants to make the cheerleading squad, but is really having a hard time. What can you say to her to encourage her not to give up.

Perseverance

16 What is the relationship between perseverance and success?

Higher-Level Thinking Questions for Character Development
Kagan Publishing • 1 (800) 933-2667 • www.KaganOnline.com

Perseverance

Journal Writing Question

Write your response to the question below.
Be ready to share your response.

If you are trying to accomplish a goal and feel like giving up, what are some things you can tell yourself to persevere?

Perseverance

Question Starters

Use the question starters below to create complete questions.
Send your questions to a partner or to another team to answer.

1. Why might quitting

2. How long

3. Would you keep trying

4. Have you ever

5. Would you give up if

6. What is the difference

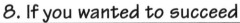
7. How could you describe

8. If you wanted to succeed

Higher-Level Thinking Questions for Character Development
Kagan Publishing • 1 (800) 933-2667 • www.KaganOnline.com

Respect

higher-level thinking questions

"The most universal quality is diversity.

— Montaigne

 # Respect
Question Cards

Respect

1 What does it mean to treat someone with respect? What things do you do? What things do you say?

Respect

2 The best way to earn respect is to treat others with respect. Do you agree or disagree? Explain your position.

Respect

3 Your class is having a discussion about explorers. A classmate says if he was an explorer, he would kill all the people and steal their valuables. It is your turn to speak. You disagree. How could you disagree respectfully?

Respect

4 If someone doesn't treat you with the respect you deserve, would you treat them with respect? Why or why not?

Respect

5 You sit down for dinner with your family and your dad serves you a big plate of spinach and mushroom pasta. Spinach makes your teeth feel funny and mushrooms make you want to puke. How can you respectfully tell your dad you don't like the dinner?

Respect

6 What would happen if no one respected anyone else?

Respect

7 A kid in your class is a babbler. He'll talk to anyone about anything and he doesn't get a clue that sometimes no one's interested. He starts talking to you in class while you're trying to do your assignment. How can you respectfully tell him to be quiet?

Respect

8 Should you treat everyone with equal respect or should you give more respect to some? Explain.

Higher-Level Thinking Questions for Character Development
Kagan Publishing • 1 (800) 933-2667 • www.KaganOnline.com

Respect
Question Cards

Respect

9 An old lady who lives across the street from you says she will pay you to help her weed her lawn. You work for three hours and do most of the work. When you're all done, she says "Thank you," smiles, and gives you three quarters. You feel ripped off. What do you do?

Respect

10 What is self-respect? Do you have a lot or a little self-respect? How do you show your self-respect?

Respect

11 Do you expect people to treat you with respect? What do you expect of strangers you meet?

Respect

12 Much of the conflict and violence we see today is from the simple lack of respect. How can we teach people to be more respectful of one another?

Respect
Question Cards

Respect

13 Who do you respect most? What are the reasons you respect him or her most?

Respect

14 Is using aggression ever a good way to gain respect? Why or why not?

Respect

15 You are playing basketball with a group of kids. One kid on your team gets mad at a kid on the other team and calls him a racist name.
You know he is being disrespectful. What do you say or do?

Respect

16 Do you consider yourself a respectful person? Why or why not?

Higher-Level Thinking Questions for Character Development
Kagan Publishing • 1 (800) 933-2667 • www.KaganOnline.com

Respect

Journal Writing Question

Write your response to the question below.
Be ready to share your response.

If someone doesn't treat you with the respect you deserve, would you treat them with respect? Why or why not?

_____
_____
_____
_____
_____
_____
_____
_____
_____
_____
_____
_____
_____
_____
_____
_____
_____

Respect

Question Starters

Use the question starters below to create complete questions.
Send your questions to a partner or to another team to answer.

1. Why is politeness

2. How would you feel if

3. Who deserves

4. Do you respect

5. If you wanted respect

6. How courteous

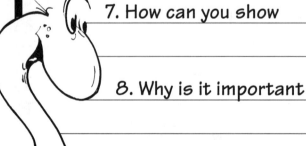

7. How can you show

8. Why is it important

Higher-Level Thinking Questions for Character Development
Kagan Publishing • 1 (800) 933-2667 • www.KaganOnline.com

Responsibility

higher-level thinking questions

To be a man is to be responsible. It is to feel shame at the sight of what seems to be unmerited misery. It is to take pride in a victory won by one's comrades. It is to feel, when setting one's stone, that one is contributing to the building of the world.

— Antoine de Saint-Exupéry

Higher-Level Thinking Questions for Character Development
Kagan Publishing • 1 (800) 933-2667 • www.KaganOnline.com

Responsibility
Question Cards

Responsibility

1 Complete the following sentence. "Responsibility is…"

Responsibility

2 You are baby-sitting your neighbors' little kids. You're roughhousing and giving them piggyback rides through the house. You accidentally break a nice vase and water spills all over. What do you do?

Responsibility

3 "With rights come responsibilities." What does this mean?

Responsibility

4 Your mom asks you to clean your room. You forget. In a disappointed voice she says, "I thought I asked you to clean your room." What do you say? Why?

Responsibility
Question Cards

Responsibility

5 On a scale of 1 to 10, how responsible would you say you are?

Responsibility

6 You join a soccer team. You practice every Monday, Wednesday, and Friday. On Wednesday, you don't feel like going to practice? Do you have a responsibility to go?

Responsibility

7 What responsibilities do you have at home?

Responsibility

8 You make plans with your friend to meet at the movies at six o'clock. You accidentally forget about your plans and go out with another friend. At eight o'clock that night you see your first friend who you were supposed to meet at the movies. She's really mad. Do you give an excuse or tell the truth?

Higher-Level Thinking Questions for Character Development
Kagan Publishing • 1 (800) 933-2667 • www.KaganOnline.com

Responsibility

9 Do you think parents should be held responsible for things their kids do? Why or why not?

Responsibility

10 Your friend invites you to his birthday party. All your friends are going. You really want to go too. When you ask your mom, she says, "Sorry, but we're going to Grandma's that weekend." What do you do?

Responsibility

11 What commitments have you made in your life?

Responsibility

12 A friend tells you a secret and makes you promise not to tell anyone. His secret is that he is going to run away. You fear for his safety. Would you keep your promise or tell his parents?

Responsibility
Question Cards

Responsibility

13 If you made a deal with someone and they did not hold up their end of the bargain, would you? Why or why not?

Responsibility

14 Can we ever really be responsible for what someone else does? Explain.

Responsibility

15 What is your greatest responsibility? Explain why it's so important.

Responsibility

16 Your parents are going away for the weekend. They ask you to take care of the house and your little brother. Your friends find out you have the house to yourself. They want you to have a party. What do you do?

Higher-Level Thinking Questions for Character Development
Kagan Publishing • 1 (800) 933-2667 • www.KaganOnline.com

Responsibility

Journal Writing Question

Write your response to the question below.
Be ready to share your response.

What is your greatest responsibility? Explain why it's so important.

_____

_____

_____

_____

_____

_____

_____

_____

_____

_____

_____

_____

_____

_____

_____

_____

_____

_____

_____

_____

Responsibility
Question Starters

Use the question starters below to create complete questions.
Send your questions to a partner or to another team to answer.

1. Who would be responsible if

2. If you were responsible for

3. What would you do if

4. How dependable

5. What's the significance

6. What responsibilities

7. Would you rather

8. What commitments

Higher-Level Thinking Questions for Character Development
Kagan Publishing • 1 (800) 933-2667 • www.KaganOnline.com

Values and Morals

higher-level thinking questions

The moral virtues, then, are produced in us neither by nature nor against nature. Nature, indeed, prepares in us the ground for their reception, but their complete formation is the product of habit.

— Aristotle

Higher-Level Thinking Questions for Character Development
Kagan Publishing • 1 (800) 933-2667 • www.KaganOnline.com

Values and Morals
Question Cards

Values and Morals

1 If your mom was dying from a terrible illness and you had no money to buy the medicine she needed, would you steal it? Why or why not?

Values and Morals

2 If you found a wallet that had $159 and a driver's license, what would you do?

Values and Morals

3 At the movie theater, your friend pulls the fire alarm. The manager sees you together by the alarm and grabs you both. He says you are in big trouble. Do you tell him your friend did it or do you get in trouble too? Why?

Values and Morals

4 If you were getting an F in math, but needed one good score to get a D, would you cheat on your math test?

Values and Morals
Question Cards

Values and Morals

5 You sell prescription drugs for a pharmaceutical company. You make more money when doctors prescribe more expensive drugs. A doctor asks you, "Why should I prescribe the more expensive drug if I don't know if it's any better than the generic brand?" You don't know if it's better. What do you say?

Values and Morals

6 If you gave the cashier a $10 bill and she gave you change for a $20, would you tell her? Is not telling different than stealing?

Values and Morals

7 You are in the sporting goods store shopping for a new soccer ball. You have $15 to spend. The ball you really want costs $35. A cheaper ball is only $14. You notice you can easily switch the price tags. Would you switch the prices? Why or why not?

Values and Morals

8 People have different beliefs about what is right or wrong, good or bad, acceptable or unacceptable. How do you decide where you stand? Give an example.

Higher-Level Thinking Questions for Character Development
Kagan Publishing • 1 (800) 933-2667 • www.KaganOnline.com

Values and Morals
Question Cards

9 You own a restaurant. A regular customer is very rude with your servers. One server accidentally spills water on him. Your customer gets angry and says he will never return unless you fire the server. What do you do?

10 This morning you have a very important test, but are running late. You pedal your bike as fast as you can. A cat runs in front of you and you run it over and kill it. If you try to find the owner to tell him or her, you'll probably miss your test. What do you do?

11 You are playing baseball in the park. You hit the ball into a nearby house window and it shatters. Everyone you're with scatters. What do you do?

12 You are with a group of friends in the mall. You all want to eat lunch together. You and half of your group want pizza. The other half, including the boy or girl you have a crush on, wants hot dogs. You hate hot dogs. He or she whispers to you, "Change your mind and we can eat together." What do you do?

Values and Morals
Question Cards

Values and Morals

13 What does it mean to have "high morals"? Do you have "high morals"?

Values and Morals

14 What is the worst thing someone could do? Why?

Values and Morals

15 Rank the following from 1 to 5, 1 being the most important to you: Honesty, Imagination, Empathy, Humor, Courage. Explain your ranking.

Values and Morals

16 Are morals absolute or relative? Absolute means they are either right and wrong regardless of the situation. Relative means they depend on things like the time, place, culture.

Higher-Level Thinking Questions for Character Development
Kagan Publishing • 1 (800) 933-2667 • www.KaganOnline.com

Values and Morals
Journal Writing Question

Write your response to the question below.
Be ready to share your response.

People have different beliefs about what is right or wrong, good or bad, acceptable or unacceptable. How do you decide where you stand? Give an example.

_____
_____
_____
_____
_____
_____
_____
_____
_____
_____
_____
_____
_____
_____
_____
_____
_____
_____

Values and Morals
Question Starters

Use the question starters below to create complete questions.
Send your questions to a partner or to another team to answer.

1. What if everyone

2. Would you say

3. How do you feel

4. How would your mother rate

5. What would you do if

6. Do you believe

7. What do you value

8. How consistent

Higher-Level Thinking Questions for Character Development
Kagan Publishing • 1 (800) 933-2667 • www.KaganOnline.com

Notes